CITY CRITTERS
Squirrels
by Betsy Rathburn
BLASTOFF! READERS
1
BELLWETHER MEDIA • MINNEAPOLIS, MN

Blastoff! Readers are carefully developed by literacy experts to build reading stamina and move students toward fluency by combining standards-based content with developmentally appropriate text.

LEVELS

Level 1 provides the most support through repetition of high-frequency words, light text, predictable sentence patterns, and strong visual support.

Level 2 offers early readers a bit more challenge through varied sentences, increased text load, and text-supportive special features.

Level 3 advances early-fluent readers toward fluency through increased text load, less reliance on photos, advancing concepts, longer sentences, and more complex special features.

★ **Blastoff! Universe**

Reading Level

Blastoff! Beginners — Grade K → Blastoff! Readers — Grades 1–3 → Blastoff! Discovery — Grade 4

This edition first published in 2025 by Bellwether Media, Inc.

No part of this publication may be reproduced in whole or in part without written permission of the publisher. For information regarding permission, write to Bellwether Media, Inc., Attention: Permissions Department, 6012 Blue Circle Drive, Minnetonka, MN 55343.

Library of Congress Cataloging-in-Publication Data

LC record for Squirrels available at: https://lccn.loc.gov/2024035388

Text copyright © 2025 by Bellwether Media, Inc. BLASTOFF! READERS and associated logos are trademarks and/or registered trademarks of Bellwether Media, Inc.

Editor: Christina Leaf Designer: Gabriel Hilger

Printed in the United States of America, North Mankato, MN.

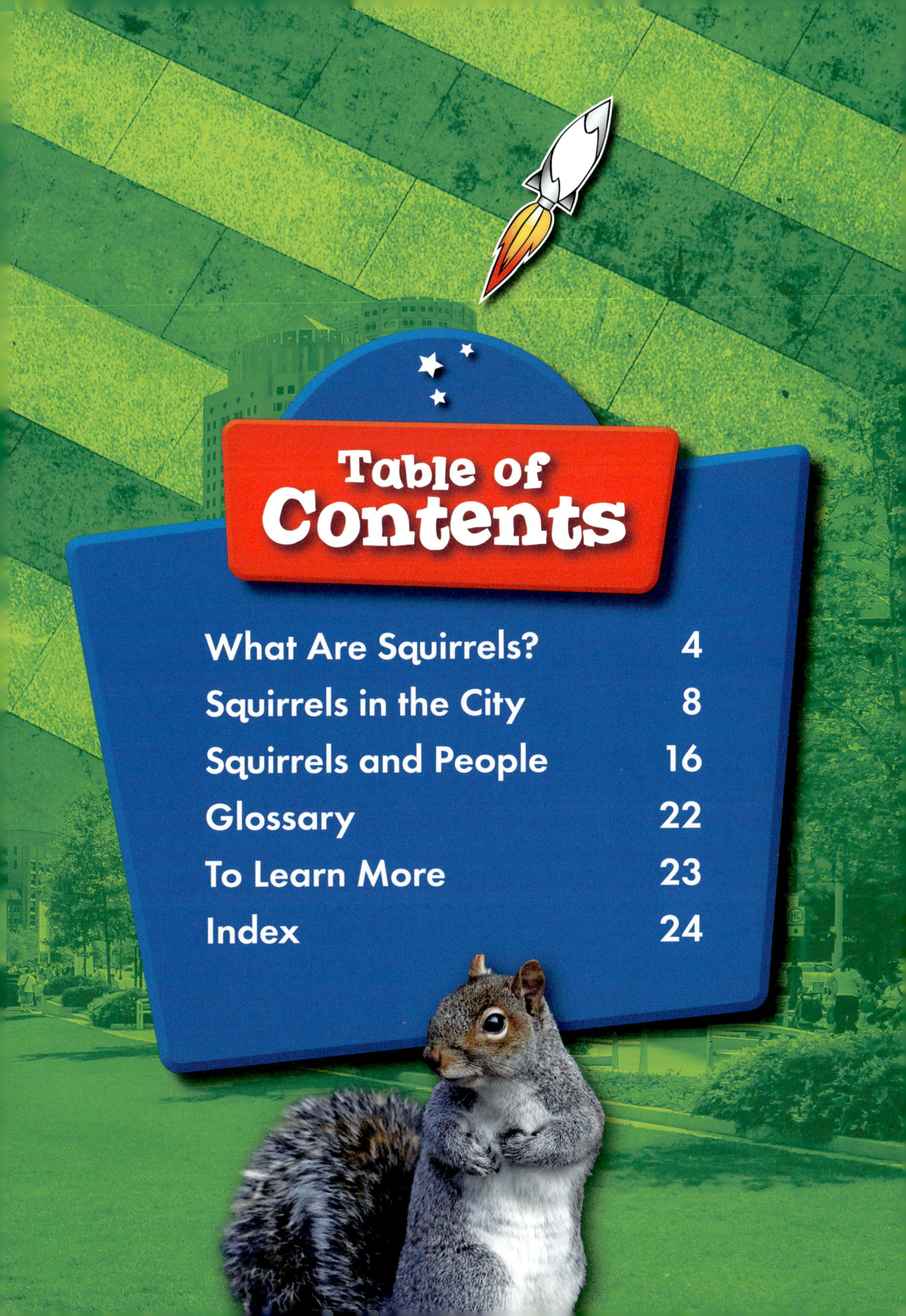

Table of Contents

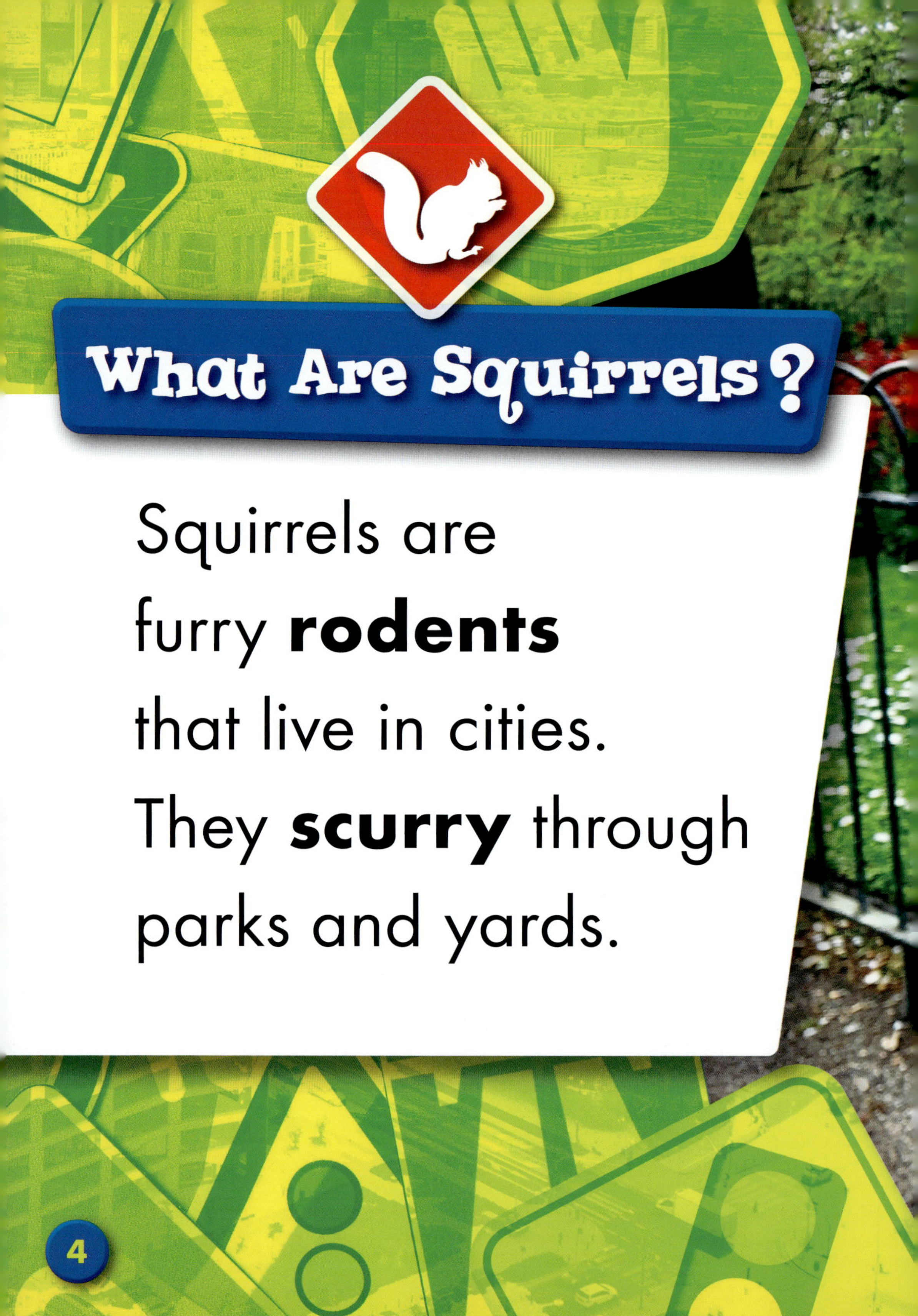

What Are Squirrels?

Squirrels are furry **rodents** that live in cities. They **scurry** through parks and yards.

They have red
or gray fur.
They have fluffy tails.

Common City Squirrels
red squirrel
gray squirrel
fox squirrel
tail

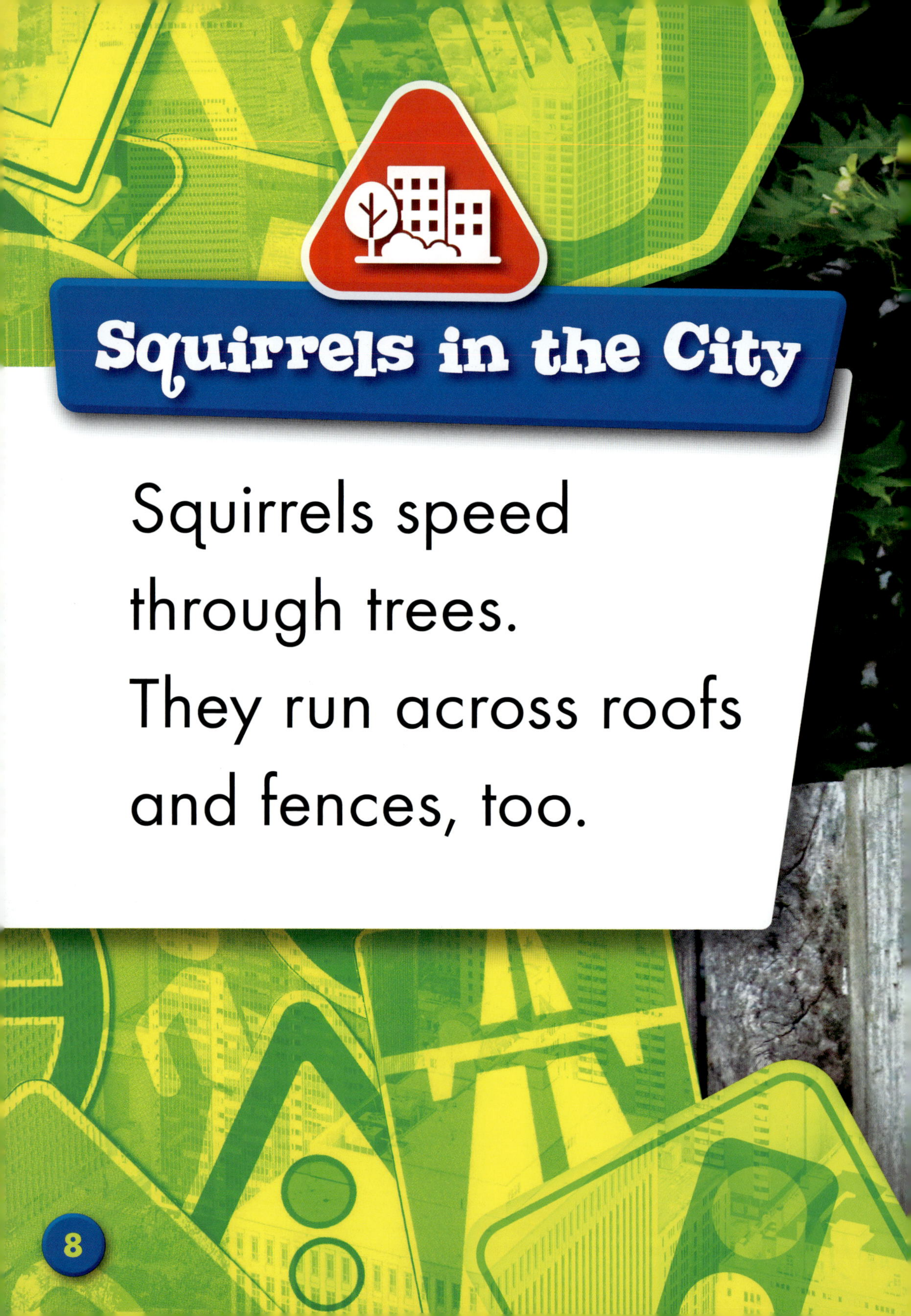

Squirrels in the City

Squirrels speed through trees. They run across roofs and fences, too.

They build nests
from leaves and sticks.
Some also use trash.

nest

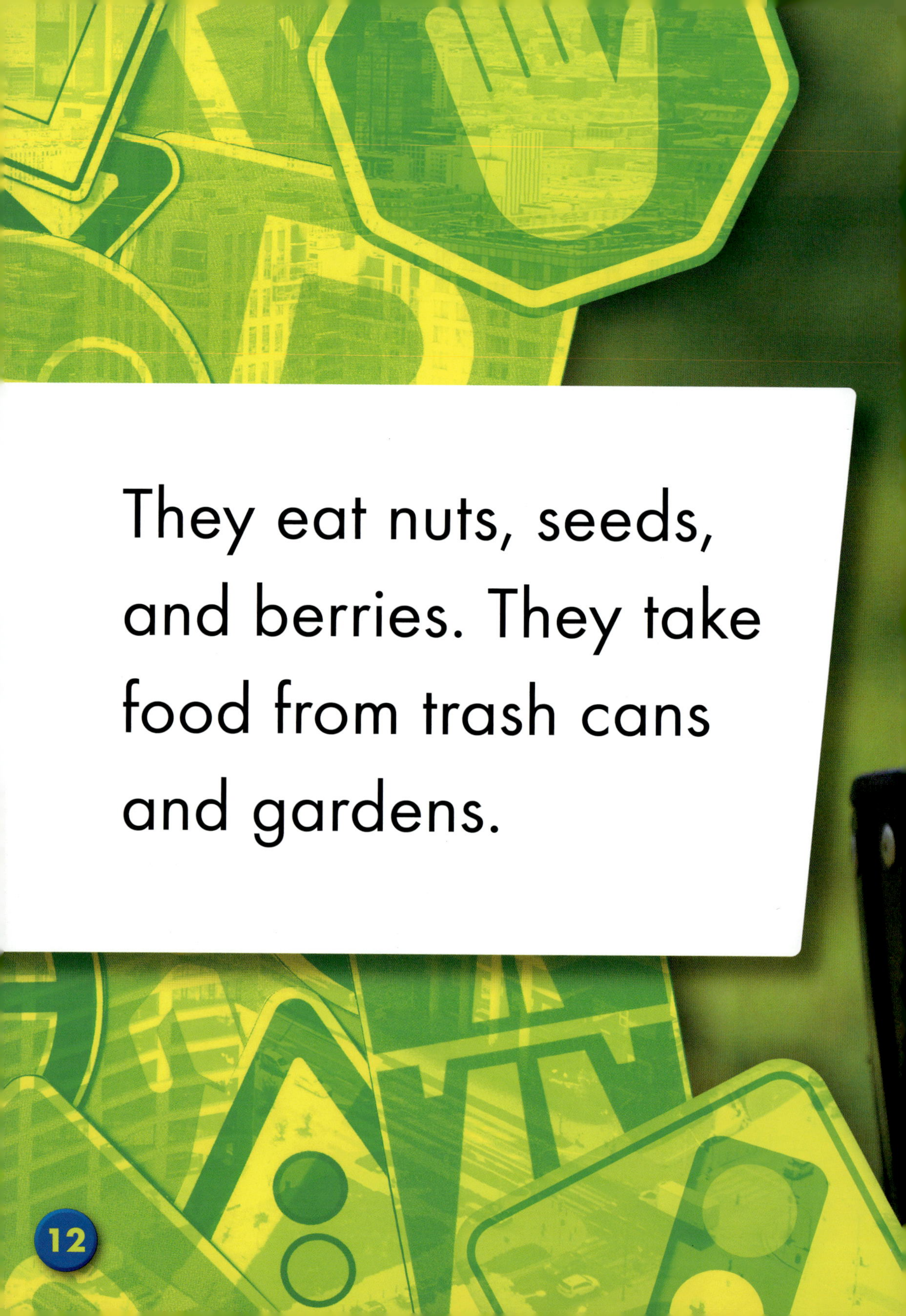

They eat nuts, seeds, and berries. They take food from trash cans and gardens.

Squirrel Food
nuts
berries
people food

They store food in **caches**. They save it for winter.

cache

Squirrels and People

Squirrels eat from bird feeders. They make homes in **attics** and sheds.

Squirrel Homes
trees
attics
sheds

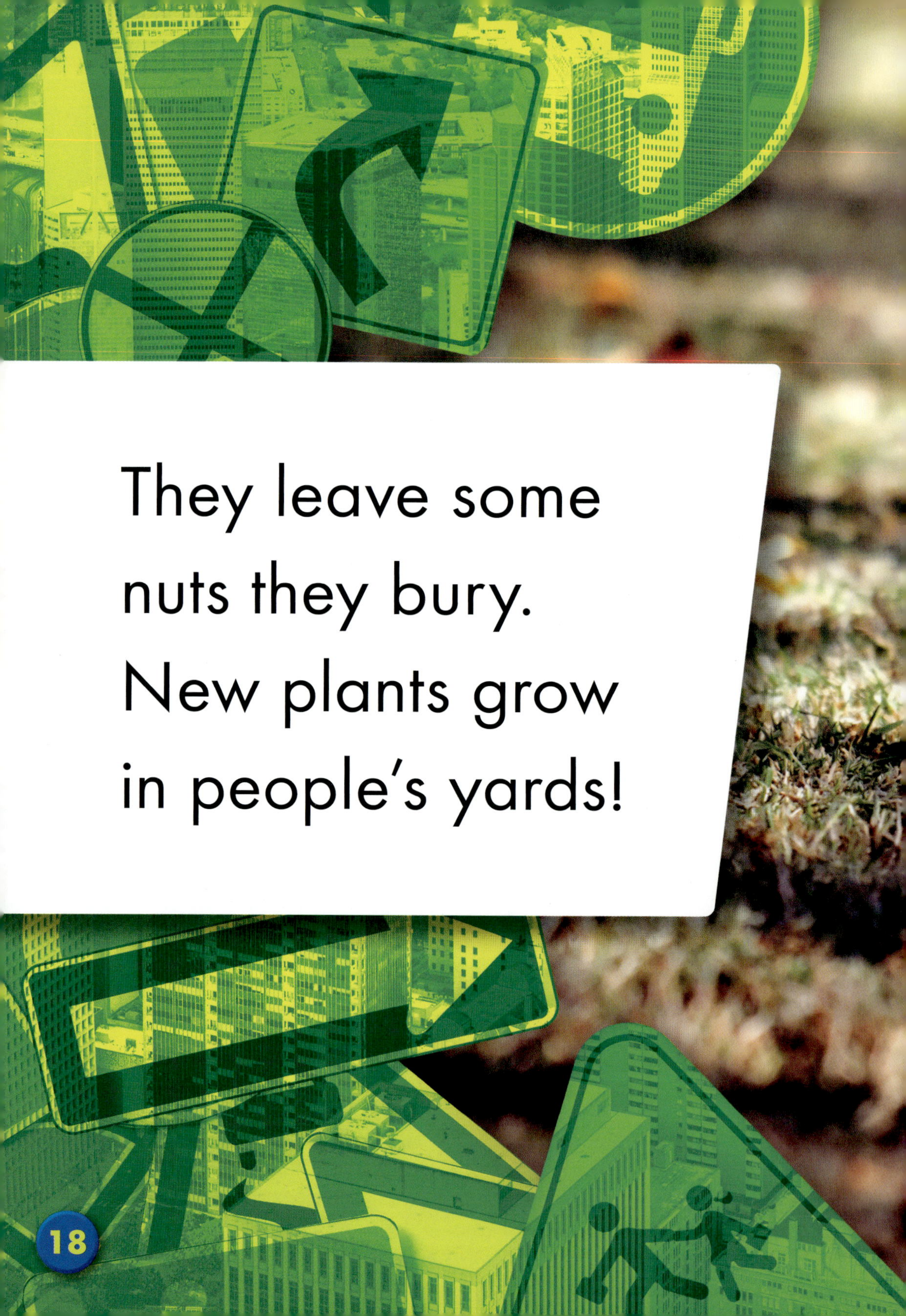

They leave some nuts they bury. New plants grow in people's yards!

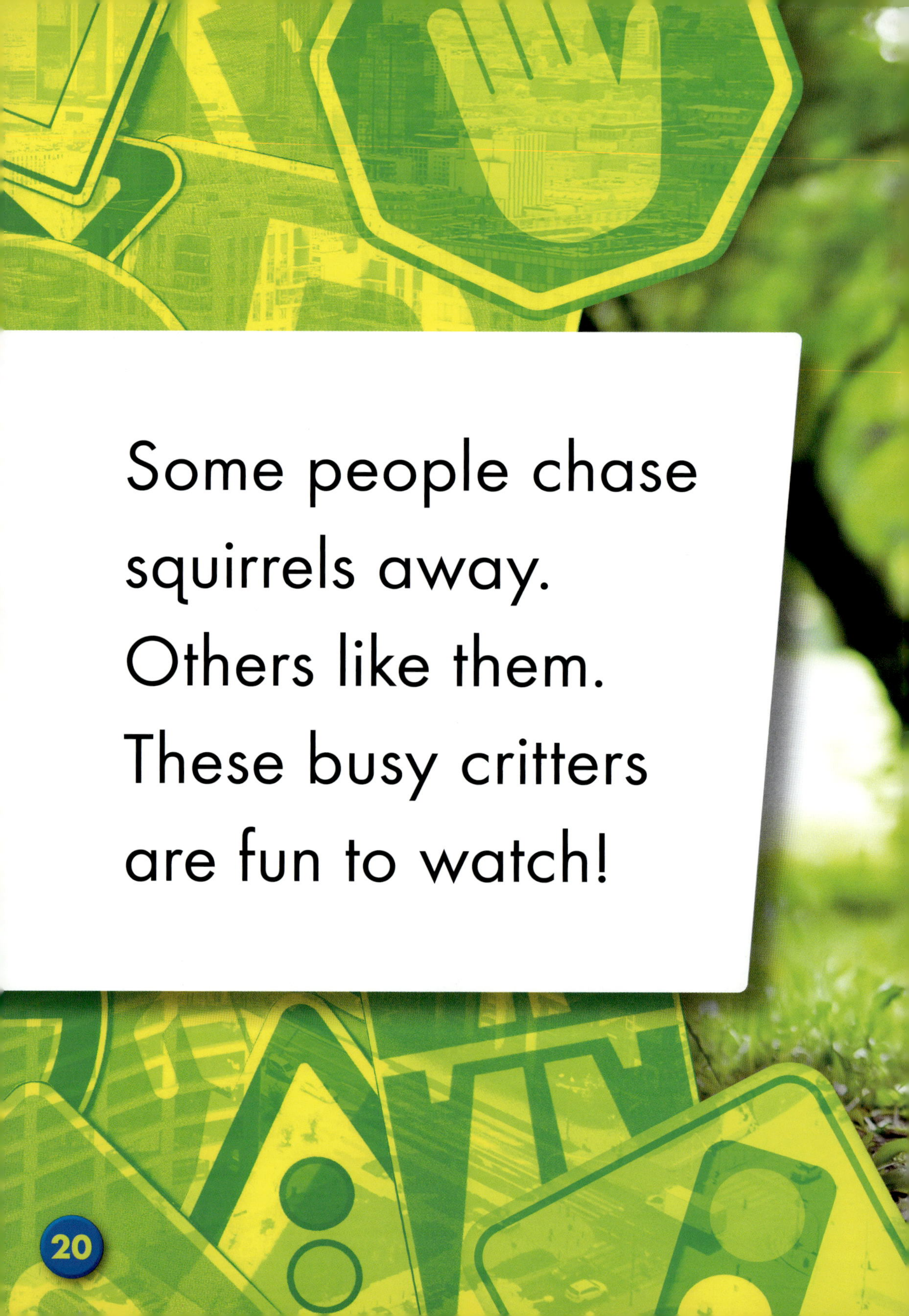

Some people chase squirrels away. Others like them. These busy critters are fun to watch!

attics

spaces below the roofs of buildings

rodents

small animals that gnaw on their food

caches

hidden places used to store food

scurry

to run with quick steps

To Learn More

AT THE LIBRARY

Carney, Elizabeth. *Animals in the City.* Washington, D.C.: National Geographic Kids, 2019.

Lee, Ashley. *Squirrels: Animals That Make a Difference!* Oliver, B.C.: Engage Books, 2021.

Zobel, Derek. *Squirrels.* Minneapolis, Minn.: Bellwether Media, 2021.

ON THE WEB

FACTSURFER

Factsurfer.com gives you a safe, fun way to find more information.

1. Go to www.factsurfer.com.
2. Enter "squirrels" into the search box and click 🔍.
3. Select your book cover to see a list of related content.

Index

The images in this book are reproduced through the courtesy of: Nigel J. Harris, front cover (squirrel); Gareth Janzen, front cover (city); Steve Midgley, p. 3; Luis Corvini Filho, pp. 4-5; Dave Turner, pp. 6-7; Brian Lasenby, p. 7 (red squirrel); IrinaK, p. 7 (gray squirrel); Bonnie Taylor Barry, p. 7 (fox squirrel); GiGi Brock, pp. 8-9; Janet Griffin, pp. 10-11; Sunshower Shots, p. 11 (nest); Pascal Huot, pp. 12-13; Auhustsinovich, p. 13 (nuts); ColorMaker, p. 13 (berries); Dr.Pixel, p. 13 (people food); Sandi Smolker, pp. 14-15; Nata.dobrovolskaya, p. 15 (cache); Mccallk69, pp. 16-17; sergey lavrishchev, p. 17 (trees); Fabrique Imagique, p. 17 (attics); Mark Seymour, p. 17 (sheds); sumikophoto, pp. 18-19; Iryna Mazorchuk, p. 19 (inset); SbytovaMN, pp. 20-21; Suzanne Tucker, p. 22 (attics); Steve Midgley, p. 22 (caches); Brownlow BioSciences, p. 22 (rodents); EMFA16, p. 22 (scurry).